AF483080

This book shares directly from my heart to
your heart. There are some pictures that
are a little less clearer than others, but
there are specific reasons for that. Some
pictures are focusing on certain things. See
if you can figure out the special meaning
behind each picture.

RES

When I was young I was told about the Savior
who could forgive all my bad behavior.

Romans 3:23- NIV
*For all have sinned and fall short of the glory of
God.*

BIBLE

I listened to my Sunday school teacher say
that Jesus would wash all my sins away.

Psalm 103:12- NIV
*As far as the east is from the west, so far has He
removed our transgressions from us.*

I longed to pray that day and have all my sins
washed away.

Romans 10:13-NIV
*Everyone who calls on the name of the Lord will be
saved.*

I didn't know just what to do. I had to really
think things through.

Proverbs 9:10-NIV
The fear of the Lord is the beginning of wisdom.

In my heart I thought about all I had been
taught and how the battle for me had already
been fought.

1 John 3:8b-NIV
*The reason the Son of God appeared was to destroy
the devil's work.*

The good news was Jesus came to this earth
to give all who would believe in Him a new
birth.

*Jesus replied, "Very truly I tell you, no one can see
the kingdom of God unless they are born again."*

You see I was lost as lost could be and
without Jesus I just couldn't see.

2 Corinthians 4:4-NIV
*The god(devil) of this age has blinded the minds of
unbelievers, so that they cannot see the light of the
gospel that displays the glory of Christ, who is the
image of God.*

See what you might ask? The truth of God at
last!!!

John 14:6-NIV
*Jesus answered, "I am the way and the truth and
the life. No one comes to the Father except through
me."*

God created us to be free and it's only in
Jesus that we can truly be.

2 Corinthians 3:16-NIV
*But whenever anyone turns to the Lord, the veil is
taken away.*

On that day I placed my full trust in him and
He washed away all my sin.

2 Corinthians 5:17-NIV
*Therefore, if anyone is in Christ, the new creation
has come: The old is gone, the new is here.*

WRONG WAY
WRONG WAY
WRONG WAY
WRONG WAY
WRONG WAY
WRONG WAY
WRONG WAY
WRO WA
16

When I got older I wandered away. But the
Lord was always in my heart to stay.

John 10:28-NIV
*I give them eternal life, and they shall never
perish: no one will snatch them out of my hand.*

WRONG WAY

The world had me convinced it was so much
fun. But chasing the things of the world
always kept me on the run.

Romans 8:13-NIV
*For if you live according to the flesh, you will die;
but if by the Spirit you put to death the misdeeds of
the body you will live.*

I longed so much to be happy and have peace
within. But I was living a life full of sin.

Psalms 32:4-NIV
*For day and night your hand was heavy on me: my
strength was sapped as in the heat of summer.*

I needed to come back to Jesus my Lord now.
Only Jesus, my savior, could show me how.

Psalms 32:5-NIV
Then I acknowledged my sin to you and did not cover up my iniquity. I said, "I will confess my transgressions to the Lord." And you forgave the guilt of my sin.

He showed me how He wanted a relationship
with me. Just spending alone time with Him
filled my heart with such glee.

Psalms 32:8-NIV
*I will instruct you and teach you in the way you
should go: I will counsel you with my loving eye on
you.*

Now I truly live each day for Him, and I don't take for granted how He washed away all my sin.

1 Thessalonians 5:18-NIV
Give thanks in all circumstances: for this is God's will for you in Christ Jesus.

Now I get up each day and say "Lord, what shall we do?" Then I say in my heart "I will follow you."

Matthew 16:24-NIV
Then Jesus said to His disciples, "Whoever wants to be my disciple must deny themselves and take up their cross and follow me."

He takes my hand to lead the way and safely
guides me each day.

Psalms 23:1-NIV
The Lord is my shepherd, I lack nothing.

I invite you to know my friend who is
knocking on the door of your heart, so you
and Him will never have to be apart.

Hebrews 13:5B-NIV
*God has said, "Never will I leave you: never will I
forsake you."*

Ask Him now to fill you full of His Holy Spirit
forever, so you two can go on this life's
adventures together.

John 14:16-NIV
*And I will ask the Father, and He will give you
another advocate to help you and be with you
forever.*

I am now a child of God forever and the life I
have left here on earth only gets better. Meet
my best friend Jesus the King. Oh what joy
and in Him I will always cling.

John 1:12-NIV
*Yet to all who did receive Him, to those who
believed in his name, he gave the right to become
children of GOD.*

BIBLE

The story doesn't end here now. Following
Jesus each day, He will show you how.

John 16:13-NIV
*But when he, the Spirit of truth, comes, he will
guide you into all the truth. He will not speak on
his own; he will speak only what he hears, and he
will tell you what is yet to come.*

When your job is done on this earth you will
flee and forever in a place called heaven with
the Lord you will be.

John 14:3-NIV
*And if I go and prepare a place for you, I will come
back and take you to be with me that you also may
be where I am.*